# Essex Girls' Limericks

## VOLUME II

# Volume II

This is the second book in celebration of Essex Girls and some of the lovely-named places where they live.

Within these pages there are girls from Lower Horse Island, Cuckingstool End and Bumbles Green, old ladies from Layer de la Haye and Ongar, a naughty girl from Cock Clarks and a good girl from Belchamp Walter, and almost 100 others.

And we have commissioned volunteers and young students from Essex schools to help illustrate this volume.

This little book fits neatly into a pocket or handbag, or even a Christmas stocking.

If you buy it you will be helping EWAG to support some of the less fortunate girls and women of Essex.

NB. All the places exist in Essex. Excluding pages 42 & 43, all characters are fictional and any similarity is purely accidental.

Books published by EWAG ~

| | | |
|---|---|---|
| Nice-Looking (Essex) Girls Afloat | ISBN 978-0-9567397-1-1 | £12.95 |
| Essex Girls' Limericks - Volume I | ISBN 978-0-9567397-0-1 | £2.95 |
| Essex Girls' Limericks - Volume II | ISBN 978-0-9567397-2-8 | £3.00 |

~

# ESSEX GIRLS and ESSEX PLACES

**Edited by:**

George Courtauld
Chairman
Essex Women's Advisory Group

~

**Published by:**

Essex Women's Advisory Group

**Copyright:**

© Essex Women's Advisory Group (EWAG) 2013

All rights reserved.

First printed and bound in the UK in 2013 by
Alphaprint (Colchester) Ltd

ISBN 978-0-9567397-2-8

A little old girl, from tiny **Twitty Fee**,
was pestered with itchments from an ENORMOUS great flea.
When staying at **Jacks Hatch**
she did scritch and did scratch,
'til advised to go drown it, at **Frinton on Sea**.

GC

Another old lady – from **Matching**
was also addicted to scratching
which she did night and day.
Her friends kept away,
**Feering** her affliction was catching.

**GC**

A dingy old maiden from **Grays**
does not have the flair to amaze:
instead of chiffons and feathers,
and boots in red leathers
she wears slippers, and garments of baize.

GC

A girl from **Lower Horse Isle**
had a lazy and languorous smile.
She said, with a dimple:
'the reason's quite simple,
the furthest I walk is a mile'.

GC

Oh! The girls from **Latchingdon-cum-Snoreham!**
How all of the fellows adore them!
With their winsome giggles,
and beguiling wriggles,
there ain't any men can ignore them.

GC

4

A chaste maiden from far **Belchamp Walter**
let her principles weaken and falter
when a Lounge Lizard fed her
and praised her, then led her
like an innocent lamb to the slaughter.

GC

Our musical Nelly from **Orsett**
had a tom-tit that dwelt in her corset
Singing at 'Songs of Praise'
in the choir, she'd amaze
hitting top 'C' – with no need to force it.

GRG

A plain maid from **Greenstead-juxta-Ongar**
went off to the Island of Tonga.
There, she said, quite smugly:
*'I'm now far from **Ugley**,
here's a place where I'll linger much longer'.*

GC

Out walking from **Beaumont-cum-Moze**
poor Josephine shivered and froze.
The most probable reason
why she was sneezin' and freezin' -
she'd forgotten to put on her clothes.

GC

By **The Peb** there lives a small witch
who dwells in a bog by a ditch;
she used to be pretty
but now, what a pity,
she's got warts, rotten teeth and an itch!

CR

Another small witch, from **Old Heath**,
was lumbered with really weird teeth:
there was one at the back
and the front ones were black
when they fell out t'was such a relief!

PT

So this lady who came from **Old Heath**
ended up with only three teeth:
the one at the back,
she used to call Jack,
whilst the front two were Robin, and Keith.

GC

A rather stout lady, from **Ugley**,
wrapped up in a very large rug, she
swathed bosoms and tum,
her legs and her bum
saying: *'it's ever-so warm and fits snugly'*.

GC

A riverboat cook on the **Twizzle**
when told not to 'drown' but to 'drizzle'
pursed her old lips
saying, *"It makes soggy the chips
and you can't hear the cheeseburgers sizzle."*

MN

When Jane was at sea in a yacht, she
felt ill, she felt sick, she felt hot, she
cried out in fear:
*'I wish I weren't here,
I want to go home, to **Black Notley**!'*

GC

A skittish young girl from **Cock Clarks**
is known for high jinks and low larks:
she is jolly and hearty;
she will romp at a party
till her underclothes shimmer with sparks.

GC

A couple from **Hanningfield Water**
had an idle and dim-witted daughter.
Her teacher said: *'look*
*you must learn from this book'.*
*She didn't, but shouldn't she oughter?*

GC

'Midst the leafy green banks of **The Crouch**
our Nellie cried out with an *'ouch!*
*I've rolled on a nettle.*
*I'd rather we'd settle*
*'midst the soft, bolstered arms of your couch!'*

GC

A greedy Girl Guide, from **Canewdon**,
found a juicy fat duck, which she stewed on
an open camp fire;
then, mad with desire
she snatched at a leg which she chewed on.

GC

A bluestocking from **Wendens Ambo**
became so enamoured of Rimbaud
in a fit of tristesse
she set fire to her dress
for a Season in Hell as a flambeau.

MN

Plump Pansy, who lives in **Wrabness**,
once wore her young sister's small dress:
the shape of her thighs
caused favourable cries,
but the size of her bum rather less.

GC

**but now**

Slim Pansy who lives near the **Stour**
said: *'I seemed to have gained my allure*
*my bum and my thighs*
*are of minuscule size*
so my friends exclaim *"blimey!"* and *"cor!!"*

PC

You're plump and you're fair, **Daisy Green**,
as pretty as any girl seen;
on your bosoms there dangles
some lovely gold bangles:
not to left, not to right, but between.

GC

In **Manuden-with-Quendon-and-Rickling**
poor Susie's wool jumper is tickling.
To get her mind off the itch
she has a good hobby which
involves baking, and roasting and pickling.

GC

It was silly of Sally to send
coy notes to her spooky pen friend:
he arrived in a parcel
which he'd mailed from his castle,
and she came to a dire **Beazley End**.

GC

The girls from **Bobbingworth Green**
take baths to keep themselves clean;
at **Havering-atte-Bower**
they usually shower
as part of their daily routine.


Along the mud banks of **The Twizzle**
their showers are no more than a drizzle,
but in **Wendens Ambo**
there's a much better flow
and so hot that it makes their skins sizzle.


Bathing is brief in **Coldharbour**,
where the chilly sea waters quell ardour,
but in **Hatfield Broad Oak**
they gracefully soak
'midst the flowers and the scents of an arbour.

GC

An elegant lady from **Stock**
shuns scruffy blue jeans for a frock;
she plays bridge in the noon,
but is planning, quite soon
to try something naughty, to shock.

PT

An old lady of **Layer de la Haye**
went out for a ramble one day,
She became a bit lost
as her eyeballs were crossed,
and finished – beside **Bathside Bay**.

GC

A girl from **Kirby-le-Soken**
cried: *'My heart is utterly broken,*
*my boyfriend has left*
*me alone and bereft*
*but for a blue-eyed blonde babe as a token'.*

GC

The wife of a **Colne** cattle king
Said: *"This weather is freezing my bling!*
*Let us fly to a place*
*where the sun warms my face*
*and we'll dance and canoodle and sing"*

PC

Two ugly old women from **Fordham**
went out for a walk, 'til it bored them.
On the way back
a sex maniac
jumped out from a bush – and ignored them.

**MF**

Whilst powerfully rowing, down **The Ching**,
our Tracy's new garters went 'ping!'
(her work with the oars
caused her hose snag her drawers).
*'Ow!'* she said: *'don't that sting!'*

GC

'What's that, butch lady of **Messing**?
A rugby shirt that you are pressing!
And why wear boots,
with pin-striped suits?'
Are you really that keen on cross-dressing?'

GC

A libidinous widow from Ely
found Shangri-la – **Chignal Smealey**.
She said, *"Fenland is fine
for a managed decline
but Essex is more touchy-feely."*

MN

'*I'm not at all fussy or finicky*'
said a lady from old **Billericay,**
'*anything I can handle:
whether Bell, Book or Candle,
as long as it isn't too sticky.*'

GC

A feisty fair maiden from Mersea
had some really big holes in her jersey.
She said: *'I don't care,
it lets in the air,
and the boys rather like it, yer see!'*

**PT**

Said a stoic old biddy, from **Paglesham Pool**:
*'me ill-fitting teeth make me dribble and drool,*
*me legs are a-covered with wriggly blue lines*
*on account of them having some very-coarse vines,*
*and me corns are that lively they hurt something cruel,*


*'me nose is all bumbled, like a little ole spud,*
*and whenever I sneezes 'tis liable to flood,*
*I'm ever so numb in the small of me back*
*cos' me bra's now too small to take up the slack,*
*and me eyes! Just like oysters in saucers of blood.*


*Me innards go wambling whenever I eat,*
*me toes are a-shrimpled, like twigs, on my feet.*
*But what Mother Nature's imposed I'll endure,*
*and use personal efforts to make it quite sure*
*that when shopping in **Burnham** I look spritely and neat.*

**GC**

Said the girl with a peeved Pekinese:
*'He hasn't much fun when he pees,*
*he ain't much to choose,*
*only a couple of loos,*
*as we live on the **Isle of Two Trees**.'*


This girl from the **Isle of Two Trees**
was truly delightful to squeeze:
she'd a willowy waist,
and bosoms well placed,
and a couple of really nice knees.

**GC**

A lady from **Stanstead Mountfitchet**
had such a long nose she could twitch it;
but it got in the way
as she drank tea one day
so she found some clothes pegs to hitch it.

**ST**

An indolent girl from **Hook End**
to the library, for work, did they send.
There, she sat on the edge
of a voluminous ledge
and earned a small fee as a book end.

GC

A mature lady from **Heybridge Basin**
said *"Excuse me while I put a face on
for I know I look foul."*
He said *"here's my trowel"*
*"Don't tell me"* she said, *"you're a mason".*

GRG

On May Day in quiet **Bumbles Green**
they elected Val carnival Queen.
She said: *'I'm from Orsett
so kindly don't force it
this place is so quiet I could scream'.*

PC

There once was a woman from **Ongar**
who complained: *'it takes longer and longer
to make Hubby's tea,
he's so fussy, you see,
and he likes his brew stronger and stronger.*

ST

A young police girl (a cadet)
wore skimpy black stockings of net.
She said: *'I suppose,*
*some are shocked by my hose,*
*but the regular socks make me sweat.'*


The young men of **Bumpstead** would bet
on which one amongst them could get
closely arrested
and even divested
by the hands of this charming Fuzzette.

GC

A young lady cockler from **Leigh**
was caught short when cockling at sea.
While adjusting her dress
She was forced to confess
That alas, she had drunk too much tea.

GRG

This incontinent young lady from **Leigh**
Said: *'fie!'* and *'fiddle de dee!*
*The tourists and grockles*
*may mock at my cockles*
*but cockling for cockles for me!'*

GC

An heiress from **Muckingcreek Marsh**
had kisses both bristly and harsh:
tho' her father's fortune
was a favourable boon,
not so were his beard and moustache.

GC

A house-wife from old **Chignal Smealey**
made her porridge all burnt, and too mealy.
Her resigned family said:
*'let's eat corn flakes instead,*
*and put this away in the wheelie.'*

GC

Three sisters, who all lived in **Stock**
between them had only one frock;
when one was out bopping
the others went shopping;
their nudity caused quite a shock.

SP

A kangaroo slept on the couch
of a lady from **Burnham on Crouch**;
but when she went shopping
it obliged her by hopping
with all of her bags in its pouch.

PT

A dear old granny from **Ongar**
is besotted in dancing the conga;
tho' she's done it, to date,
since 1908
I think she won't do it much longer.'

GC

On the bus from **Cuckingstool End**
Sal blethered non-stop to her friend
until, as expected
she was roughly ejected:
'twas thus did her shrill **Chatter End**.

GC

From the ramparts of high **Castle Hedingham**
the maids would hang nets, with some bread in them
for the larks, tits and plovers;
but on unwanted lovers
they dropped buckets with boiling hot lead in them.

GC

Justly famed are the braw Scottish pipers
who piped at the Somme and at Ypres,
but on the battle-scarred plain
of el Alamain
piped two of the **Dagenham** Girl Pipers!

*Pipe Major Peggy Iris and Sergeant Margaret Fraser*
[Ypres was pronounced Why-pers by the Tommies]
GC

'I've adopted a chimp as my ward,'
said a kindly old girl from **Chelmsford**:
*'he arranges my flowers*
*and sings – bass – in two choirs,*
*but he always seems listless and bored.*

*'Though I bring him to* **Frinton** *to swim,*
*and take him to* **Hornchurch** *to hymn,*
*then down to* **Black Notley**
*to play with the motley,*
*there's nothing which seems to please him -*

*'neither shrimping at* **Shoeburyness**
*nor bowls on the* **Isle of Foulness**;
*at the casino of* **Southend-on-Sea**
*he just sat and searched for a flea:*
*I regret that he couldn't care less; -*

*'one evening in* **Itchycoo Park**
*I pretended to hunt for the Snark:*
*the bored chimp, refusing*
*to find it amusing*
*sat smoking his fags in the dark; -*

*'he skied down **Bread & Cheese Hill**,*
*(I hoped it would give him a thrill),*
*then to **Willingale Doe***
*to play in the snow*
*but he seemed rather tired and quite ill; -*


*we sailed round the **Island of Potton**,*
*went pub-crawling in fair **Belchamp Otten**:*
*but when reminded later*
*he yawned, as if: 'Mater,*
*those pastimes I've completely forgotten.'*


*I thought his interest I'd catch*
*if I took him to **Kelvedon Hatch***
*to see the Secret Nuclear Bunker.*
*But all he did, was to hunker*
*down and have a good scratch.*


*'Hurrah! He's become happy and good,*
*I thought that somehow he would:*
*I've found a nice place*
*to bring a smile on his face –*
*it's a hut in **Tittymouse Wood**.*

**GC**

A slimmer from **Seven Star Green**
became terribly skinny and lean:
so flat and compressed
that her back touched her chest
and sideways she couldn't be seen.

?

34

Said M'lady, on a smart horse:
*'I regret I'm a bit of a lorse,*
*where am I, young Jack?'*
*'Y're on a big 'hoss's back.'*
Cor! Wasn't that old **Countess Cross**!


(Being nobly born, the lady, of course,
pronounced 'loss' as rhymed with 'horse';
young Jack called a horse 'an hoss',
pronouncing thus the steed with 'moss').

**GC**

Bird-watching in **Pennyhole Fleet**
our Tracy would practise deceit
to encourage the birds
which arrived in great herds:
she'd cackle and twitter and tweet.

GC

A lady who lived in **Point Clear**
kept a vulgar and bad-tempered bear:
it was rude, it was crude,
having gobbled its food,
it would fart, then snigger, or swear.

It remained unseemly and rude
when she moved to live by **The Strood**.
The lady who owned it,
finally disowned it
when it danced on the beach in the nude

**GC**

An **Es-sex**y mechanic, Rosanna,
Wears tight overalls and a bandana;
She'll sashay to the bench
Pick up a torque wrench
And tighten your nuts with a spanner.

**GRG**

A bristly young maiden from **Dedham**
regretfully admitted: *'that I'm*
*Inclined to surmise*
*that the hairs on my thighs*
*so erode on my tights, that they shred 'em.'*

GC

There was a prudent maiden, she came from **Theydon Bois**
and of the chaps who courted her she quickly made her choice:
tho' her inclinations were to like
the jolly one with an old push-bike
she chose the one with spectacles –
but a natty new Rolls Royce.

GC

There was a naughty damsel, she lived by **Birdbrook Mill**,
she always was a-fidget, never was she still.
Her agile undulations
caused masculine laudations,
there were otters in the water, but she was 'otter still.

GC

With a low, and a slow and a soft sultry murmur,
sexily speaks our Susan from **Sturmer**,
bur when leading the Guides, as Brown Owl
[or some similar fowl]
her voice becomes firmer and sterner.

GC

Sal saw a wee fly on a wall
and asked: *'why didn't it fall?*
*'Perhaps its feet stuck,*
*perhaps it was luck,*
*perhaps gravity misses things small?'*

?

41

From **Leigh on Sea** she came
And swiftly she gained great acclaim
Though often she has been
Mistaken for the Queen
Helen Mirren is really a Dame!

DF

Our patron. Vicki Michelle
Was born and raised in **Chigwell**
Though seen on your set
As French waitress Yvette
She's really a great Essex girl!

DF

From **Harlow** you'd think this Posh girl
Was going for a date with an earl.
To The Castle she went
But her life has been spent
With a guy who can make a ball curl.

DF

'Turn It Up Louder, Mama Do'
Sang the girl from **Brentwood** and who
Has talent – what a Lott
This Essex girl's got
Just shows what a Pixie can do!

DF

A mother-to-be from **Foxearth**
had cravings before she gave birth:
she ate tons of pork pies,
cream cakes and French fries
which rapidly tripled her girth.

GC

44

Diana from rural **Great Leighs**
found her dog was infested with fleas.
She immersed it in Jeyes
for a couple of days;
then she allowed it to sit on her knees.

**PC**

Two old ladies, called Mildred and Sue,
were embarrassed at **Colchester** zoo
when the monkey they'd spied
exposed its backside
all mottled in purple and blue.

So the ladies in **Colchester** zoo
went off to examine the gnu.
*'Sue, look at its eyes,*
*with unease I surmise*
*that the gnu is watching us, too.'*

But they continued to discuss and to view
the various parts of the gnu.
Then off they hurried
flustered and worried
when the gnu gave a scowl and said *'BOO!'*

Sue said, as they walked round the zoo:
*'Cor, look at that old cockatoo!'*
The cockatoo said:
*'that hat on your head*
*is made from someone I knew.'*

Mildred said, as they carried on through:
*'I reckon this bird's an emu.'*
Then a notice they read
and it said, that instead
WE NAME
THIS 'ERE BIRD
AN 'OOPOO

At the cage of some old Caribou
Sue said: *'Oh blimey! Oh phoo!*
*this smell is as ripe*
*as my Hubby's old pipe*
*or maybe his socks, or his shoe.'*

Some bears, in the **Colchester** zoo
were *'at it'*, in full public view.
*'Stop 'em!'* Sue said,
*'give 'em buns, or some bread!'*
*'Stop for buns!'* said the Keeper. *'would you?*

**GC**

A plump little piggy from **Wix**
built a cosy, warm sty out of sticks;
then a wolf came along,
with a smile and a song:
'twere better she'd built it from bricks.

GC

A piggy from **Wicken Bonhunt**
was born as a tiny wee runt,
to make her feel big
this little old pig
developed a booming great grunt.

This sonorous grunting did send
her farmer, with wrath, round the bend;
at last, in his ire
he sent the sow to expire
at that hamlet of doom – **Bacon End**.

GC

A gentleman farmer from **Colne**
had a very small dachshund called Joan.
The neighbour's Great Dane
met her out in the lane.
It said *"What a fabulous bone!"*

**PC**

A large lady from **Messing-cum-Inworth**
had a pug-dog of similar girth;
when it sat on her knees
they did gasp and did wheeze,
and panted for all they were worth.

GC

Having seen a fair belle from **East Mersea**
Ron rapidly ripped off his jersey.
At the sight of Ron's passion
the damsel turned Ashen
and cried out: *'oh blimey, oh mercy!'*

GC

# Writers

| | |
|---|---|
| CR | Candida Robson |
| DF | Daphne Field |
| GC | George Courtauld |
| GRG | Geoff Russell Grant |
| MF | Martin French |
| MN | Martin Newell |
| PC | Pansy Cooper |
| PT | Peter Thistlethwayte |
| ST | Sarah Thistlethwayte |
| ? | Anonymous |

# Artists

| | | |
|---|---|---|
| AL | Alexandra Lazar | cyanworks@gmail.com, |
| AS | Abbie Street | Billericay School |
| MM | Marianne Murray | Billericay School |
| JB | Jean Baxter | |
| TS | Taylor Smith | Greensward Academy, Hockley |
| SW | Sam Winter | Greensward Academy, Hockley |

**The purpose of the Essex Women's Advisory Group [EWAG] is to support the well-being of Essex women and girls by –**

- promoting self-esteem in Essex females by giving them pride in their county and their county compatriots;

- addressing the needs of young (14 to 30) Essex females in need of help;

- teaching and training in commerce, the arts and sports;

- creating the Essex Girls' Fund, an endowed fund, also administered by the ECF, to assist

    a) Essex-based female charities and

    b) to help Essex females to be successful in business;

The method is to use the resources of a group of concerned people, both professional and volunteer. Resources include membership of apt bodies (e.g. Police, Prince's Trust, probation, Girlguiding, the WI); and/or experience, expertise, personal commitment and concern.

For more information, to buy books and articles, and to offer funds, contact EWAG at

### www.essexwomensadvisorygroup.com

The Essex Rural Fund and the Essex Girls Fund
are administered by the Essex Community Foundation
Reg. Charity No. 1052061

Some of the charities to whom EWAG has made donations to date include the Rape and Crisis Centre; Women's Refuges – Safer Places; the Prince's Trust in Essex – Development Awards for females; Girl Guiding in Essex.